# Make Yourself a Monster

MAKE YOURSELF

# A Book of Creepy Crafts

# A MONSTER!

By
Kathy Ross

Illustrated by
Sharon Hawkins Vargo

THE MILLBROOK PRESS
Brookfield, Connecticut

For my
favorite little monster
—all grown up—
Greyson.

KR

For my monster guys
— Chris, Ryan, Scott,
Craig, and Kevin.
With ♡

SV

Library of Congress Cataloging-in-Publication Data
Ross, Kathy (Katharine Reynolds), 1948-
Make yourself a monster!: a book of creepy crafts /
by Kathy Ross ; illustrated by Sharon Hawkins Vargo.
p.  cm.
Summary: Provides instructions for twenty craft projects with
a monster theme, created using common household materials.
ISBN 0-7613-1556-X (lib. bdg.). — ISBN 0-7613-1049-5 (pbk.)
1. Handicraft—Juvenile literature.  2. Monsters in art—Juvenile
literature.  [1. Handicraft.  2. Monsters in art.]
I. Vargo, Sharon Hawkins, ill.  II. Title.
TT160.R714236  1999
745.5—dc21  98-50751  CIP  AC


Published by The Millbrook Press, Inc.
2 Old New Milford Road
Brookfield, Connecticut 06804
Visit us at our Web Site — http://www.millbrook.com

# Contents

# Creeping Metal Hand

## HERE IS WHAT YOU NEED:

aluminum foil

scissors

12-inch (30-cm) pipe cleaner

masking tape

two wooden beads

## HERE IS WHAT YOU DO:

**1** Shape the aluminum foil around your fingers and hand to make the creeping hand shape. Do not make the foil so tight that you cannot slip the metal hand on and off your own hand.

6

Cut two small slits on
the top side of the hand.
Bend the pipe cleaner in half
and then fold each end in to the
center. Slip one folded end of the
pipe cleaner through one slit and out
the other so that the ends stick evenly out of each side of
the top of the hand. These will be the eye stems.

**3**

Reinforce the center of the foil between the two
pipe cleaner ends with some strips of
masking tape. Add
one or more
layers of foil
to the hand to
hide the tape.

**4**

Slide a bead onto the end of each
eye stem. If necessary, bend the
doubled end of the stem to hold
the bead in place.

7

Slide your own hand into
the metal hand to activate
the "creeping metal hand."
. . . eek!

Make this mask that wails like a banshee.

# Howling Banshee Mask

## HERE IS WHAT YOU DO:

**1** Cut several ½-inch (1-cm) slits around the end of the party horn and bend the slits out from the rim of the horn.

**2** Just inside the rim of both paper plates, cut a hole that is the same size as the open end of the party horn, so that the holes align with each other.

## HERE IS WHAT YOU NEED:

scissors

cardboard party horn

stapler

two 9-inch (23-cm) paper plates

newspaper to work on

gray and red poster paint

paintbrush

marker

nine or more 12-inch (30-cm) black pipe cleaners

hole punch

white glue

white and black construction-paper scraps

**3** Put the blower end of the horn through the hole from the back of one of the plates until the cut slits rest on the plate. Cover the plate with the second plate, lining up the cut holes. Staple the plates together. Staple the tabs to hold the horn in place.

**4** Paint the mask gray or any other color to give it an unhealthy look. Paint the area around and inside the horn red to look like a mouth. Let the paint dry before continuing.

**5** Cut eyes from the construction paper scraps and glue them above the mouth. Use a marker to draw a nose.

**6** Punch nine or more holes around the top and sides of the face. Thread a pipe cleaner through each hole and twist it around itself just above the hole to hold it in place. Bend each piece of pipe cleaner into waves to resemble hair sticking out from the face of the banshee.

Make your banshee howl and moan on a dark night.

Wrap your own mummy.

# Mummy Pin

## HERE IS WHAT YOU NEED:

wooden
ice-cream spoon

white glue

old white sneaker lace

two small
wiggle eyes

Styrofoam
tray for drying

safety pin or piece of
sticky-back magnet

## HERE IS WHAT YOU DO:

**1** Rub both sides of
the wooden spoon
with glue.

**2** Wrap the entire spoon with
the sneaker lace to look like a
mummy. Tuck the end of the
lace under itself at what will be the
back of the mummy.

10

**3** Separate the lace at the bowl end of the spoon at the front of the mummy. Glue the two wiggle eyes on the spoon to look like they are peeking out through the bandages.

**4** Rub glue all over both sides of the mummy to hold the wrap. Let it dry on the Styrofoam tray.

**5** Add a safety pin to the back of the mummy to wear as a pin. To use the mummy as a magnet, press a piece of sticky-back magnet to the back.

White jersey pot-holder loops also make good wrappings for this mummy project.

11

This little monster is slimy and gross.

# Slimy Monster Mitt Puppet

## HERE IS WHAT YOU NEED:

two zip-to-close sandwich bags

scissors

hair gel

rickrack

craft foam

## HERE IS WHAT YOU DO:

**1** Turn one of the plastic bags inside out. Place the turned bag inside the other bag so that the edges of the inner and outer bag will zip to each other.

**2** Squeeze about a cup of hair gel in the monster color of your choice into the space between the two bags. Squeeze half in on one side and half on the other to help distribute it evenly.

**3** Cut out two eyes from the craft foam. Put the eyes in between the two bags on one side.

**4** Cut a strip of rickrack for monster teeth and slip the teeth in below the eyes.

**5** Zip the two sides of the bag closed and fold the ends up to help prevent any leaks.

You might have another idea for your monster face, but don't use anything that could puncture the bag. Slip your hand into the bag to use your unusually gross mitt puppet.

13

# Big Foot's Feet

## HERE IS WHAT YOU DO:

**1** Remove the lids and turn both shoe boxes upside down. Cut a hole in the bottom end of each box, just large enough to slip your bare foot through.

**2** Cut five toes of graduating size from each shoe box lid. Glue five toes to the bottom of each shoe box, sticking off the end opposite the foot hole.

## HERE IS WHAT YOU NEED:

two shoe boxes of similar size

scissors

white glue

paper cup

brown yarn

BROWN

brown poster paint and a paintbrush

DAILY NEWS

newspaper to work on

masking tape

white Styrofoam tray

14

**3** Cut about three cups of 1-inch (2.5-cm)-long brown yarn pieces.

**4** Mix one part glue to two parts brown paint in the paper cup.

**5** Working on newspaper, paint one shoe box foot brown, including the toes. Then sprinkle the foot with brown yarn pieces to look like fur. Press the fur into the gluey paint to make sure it will stick. Paint the other foot the same way.

**6** Cut five claws for each foot from the white Styrofoam tray. Wrap the flat end of each claw with a strip of masking tape to create a better gluing surface. Glue a claw sticking out from under each toe.

Take off your shoes and slip into your new feet. Then put your shoes on again underneath the big feet. Big feet can make you very clumsy, so walk carefully and stay away from stairs.

What do you have floating around in that bottle?

# Blob in a Bottle Necklace

## HERE IS WHAT YOU DO:

**1** Fill the plastic bottle about three-quarters full of corn syrup.

**2** Color the corn syrup with a drop of green food coloring.

## HERE IS WHAT YOU NEED:

small clear plastic bottle or vial with a lid

light corn syrup

green food coloring

ruler

two small wiggle eyes

scissors

yarn

LIGHT CORN SYRUP

GREEN

16

**3** Drop in the two wiggle eyes and put the lid securely on the bottle.

**4** Cut a 3-foot (1-m) length of yarn. Tie the two ends of the yarn together to make a necklace. Slip the end of the necklace through itself and pull it tight around the neck of the plastic bottle.

Tip the bottle back and forth to move the floating eyes of the blob around. Strange . . . very strange!

17

Do you smell smoke?

# Fire-Breathing Dragon Puppet

## HERE IS WHAT YOU NEED:

small oatmeal box

adult-size green sock

white glue

scissors

four small brown pom-poms

two large white pom-poms or cotton balls

sheets of red and orange tissue paper

## HERE IS WHAT YOU DO:

**1** Remove the lid from the oatmeal box and cut out the bottom of the box.

**2** Cut the toe off the sock about 1 inch (2½ cm) from the end of the sock so that the sock is open at both ends. Save the toe piece.

Slide the sock over the oatmeal box so that the cuff end is left loose over one end of the box to form the mouth of the dragon.

 Cut the toe scrap in half so that each piece has part of the top and the bottom of the sock. Fold each piece into an ear and glue the ears sticking up from the back of the top of the head at the back.

 Glue the two large pom-poms on the head for the eyes. Glue a small brown pom-pom on each eye for the pupil.

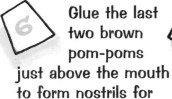 Glue the last two brown pom-poms just above the mouth to form nostrils for the dragon.

Lightly crumple a sheet of red and a sheet of orange tissue paper together. Put the crumpled paper inside the box head of the dragon.

 To make the dragon "breathe fire," put your hand up through the foot of the sock and push the tissue forward to come out of the dragon's mouth like fire.

19

# Peeking Eyes

## HERE IS WHAT YOU DO:

## HERE IS WHAT YOU NEED:

plastic wrap

cellophane tape

PINK

GREEN

YELLOW

squeeze bottles of glow-in-the-dark craft paints

**1** Tear off a square of plastic wrap and place it on a hard flat surface.

20

2 Use the glow-in-the-dark paints to draw pairs of eyes on the plastic wrap. When the paint has dried completely, stick the plastic wrap to a window. Some plastic wraps will cling to the window while others will need some tape to keep the wrap in place.

Shine a light on the paint, then turn the light out. Glowing eyes will be peering at you. Creepy!

Yikes! That house is haunted!

# Haunted House Puppet

## HERE IS WHAT YOU DO:

**1** Turn the shoe box lid on the short side to form a tall house. Cut a three-sided door and some three-sided windows in the house so the monsters can peek out.

**2** Paint the house brown and let it dry.

### HERE IS WHAT YOU NEED:

scissors

shoe box lid

BROWN

brown poster paint and a paintbrush

DAILY NEWS

newspaper to work on

black marker

GLUE

white glue

felt scraps

old knit glove

pipe cleaners

construction paper

**3** Cut a roof from the construction paper. Glue the roof to the top of the house.

**4** Use the marker to add details to the house such as window bars, shutters, a doorknob, roof shingles, and maybe a few spiders.

**5** Decorate each finger of the glove like a little monster. Use bits of felt and pipe cleaners to design your own group of monsters.

To use the haunted house puppet, hold the house in one hand and put the glove monsters on your other hand. Have your monsters pop in and out of the door and windows of the house.

BOO!

Wash in the blood of Dracula!

# Dracula Soap Dispenser

## HERE IS WHAT YOU NEED:

two pump bottles of white liquid soap

red food coloring

two rubber bands

scissors

ruler

red and black permanent markers

black trash bag

white Styrofoam tray

## HERE IS WHAT YOU DO:

**1** Color the soap in both bottles with a small amount of red food coloring to look like blood. Don't use too much!

**2** Turn both spouts to the left, then use a rubber band to hold the bottles together as shown.

24

**3** Cut a 4½-inch (11-cm) circle from the Styrofoam tray. Hold the circle in front of the two spouts. Mark on the back where the spouts should be pushed through to form the teeth. Poke a small hole through each mark.

**4** Use the markers to draw a Dracula face and hair on the Styrofoam circle.

**5** Slide the face over the two spouts so that they stick out to form the teeth.

**6** Cut a long rectangle from the trash bag and wrap it around the bottles to make a cape for Dracula. Use the second rubber band to hold the cape in place.

To use the Dracula soap dispenser, just push on the spouts behind the head and blood—I mean soap—will come out to wash your hands.

Would you like your incredible brain power to be more visible? Amaze your friends with this oversized brain.

# Giant Brain

## HERE IS WHAT YOU DO:

**1** Lightly stuff both legs of the panty hose with fiberfill. Do not overstuff the legs or they will feel very heavy to wear.

## HERE IS WHAT YOU NEED:

old pair of panty hose

FIBERFILL

fiberfill

mirror

26

**2** Pull the waistband part of the panty hose down over your head. Looking in a mirror, weave the two legs of the panty hose around each other to shape the brain on top of your head.

**3** Take the brain off and tie one leg around the other to hold the brain shape.

Your brain will probably need arranging each time you wear it. If you are feeling very intellectually superior, you might want to stuff and add another leg or two to your brain. Just weave it in and tie it to the first pair of legs. Brilliant!

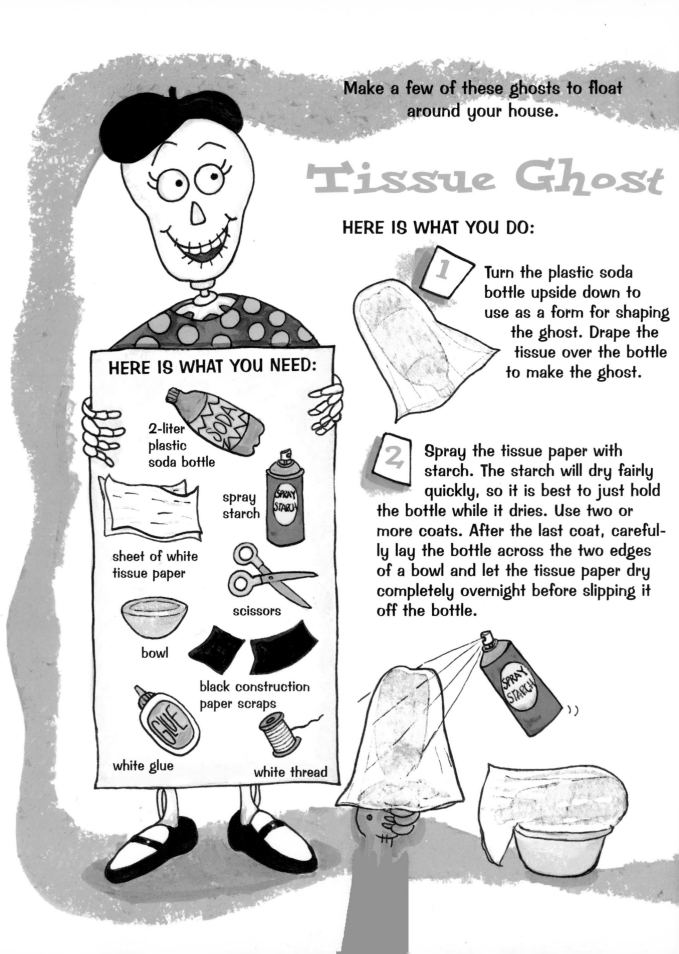

Make a few of these ghosts to float around your house.

# Tissue Ghost

## HERE IS WHAT YOU DO:

**1** Turn the plastic soda bottle upside down to use as a form for shaping the ghost. Drape the tissue over the bottle to make the ghost.

**2** Spray the tissue paper with starch. The starch will dry fairly quickly, so it is best to just hold the bottle while it dries. Use two or more coats. After the last coat, carefully lay the bottle across the two edges of a bowl and let the tissue paper dry completely overnight before slipping it off the bottle.

## HERE IS WHAT YOU NEED:

2-liter plastic soda bottle

spray starch

sheet of white tissue paper

scissors

bowl

black construction paper scraps

white glue

white thread

**3** Cut eyes for the ghost from the black construction paper and glue them in place.

**4** Glue a 3-foot (1-m) length of thread to the back of the ghost for a hanger.

Tape one or more ghosts to hang from the ceiling. These airy tissue ghosts will swing and sway at the slightest breeze. Whooooo . . .

29

Frankenstein will keep your secrets safe!

# Frankenstein Paper Keeper

## HERE IS WHAT YOU NEED:

large cereal box

masking tape

scissors

white glue

two metal bolts

light green and black construction paper

construction paper scraps in colors of your choice

markers

## HERE IS WHAT YOU DO:

**1** Tape the open top of the box closed. Cut across the front, one side, and the back of the cereal box about one third of the way down the box so that the top portion of the box will open and close from the side.

**2** Reinforce the hinge of the box with masking tape. Wrap strips of masking tape over the outer surface of the box in a random pattern to create a better gluing surface.

30

**3** Glue light green paper to cover the bottom portion of the box for Frankenstein's face. Glue black paper to the sides and top portion of the box for his hair.

**4** Poke a small hole in each side of the hair to insert a bolt so that one sticks out on each side of the head. Use tape inside the box to secure the ends of the bolts.

**5** Use the markers and cut paper scraps to make a face for Frankenstein on the front of the box.

Hide your secret stuff inside the box. Who would dare to look inside the head of Frankenstein?

TOP SECRET

31

# The Hand

## HERE IS WHAT YOU DO:

**1** Mix the plaster according to the directions on the package. You can add a few drops of food coloring to the mix. It may separate, but even streaky color will be effective.

## HERE IS WHAT YOU NEED:

disposable bowl for mixing

plaster of Paris

water

food coloring

spoon for mixing

scissors

rubber glove

**2** Pour the plaster into the glove, making sure that it goes into each finger without leaving any air space. You may want to ask someone else to hold the glove while you pour the plaster. Gently shake the glove to settle the plaster.

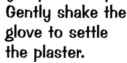

32

**3** You need to hold the glove hanging down for several minutes while the plaster sets. This takes some patience, but it is worth the effort. When the plaster feels hard, gently lay the glove on a flat surface to set overnight.

**4** It is best to clean the bowl and spoon in a bucket of water and dump it outside rather than down the drain.

**5** Carefully peel or cut the glove away from the plaster hand. If you break a finger off, don't worry about it. You can glue it back on and cover the damage with a spider ring or just leave the finger resting near the hand for a gruesome effect.

You can paint your hand, give it fake nails, and add some jewelry if you wish. This hand looks great sticking out from the center of a bowl of candy.

**33**

# Giant Reptile

## HERE IS WHAT YOU DO:

**1** Fold one plate in half to form the body of the reptile. Cut arms and legs from the two other plates by stacking them so that the two arms and the two legs are identical. Staple the arms and legs on each side of the body.

**2** Cut a long tail from the rim of a plate. Staple the tail to the back of the body.

## HERE IS WHAT YOU NEED:

five 9-inch (23-cm) paper plates

scissors

stapler

DAILY NEWS

newspaper to work on

RED GREEN
green and red poster paint and paintbrush

Styrofoam tray for drying

red party blower

black marker

34

**3** Cut a rounded head from a folded plate, leaving it attached at the fold. Cut a mouth out of the head. Staple the head over the top of the body.

**4** Paint the inside of the mouth red. Paint the rest of the reptile green. Let the reptile dry on the Styrofoam tray.

RED  GREEN

**5** Use the marker to draw slits for eyes.

**6** Slip the end of the party blower into the mouth of the reptile so that the blower sticks out behind the head. To make the tongue protrude from the head, just blow on the party blower.

What an amazing tongue!

There is something strange sticking up out of the water.

# Creep From the Deep Hat

## HERE IS WHAT YOU DO:

**HERE IS WHAT YOU NEED:**

- scissors
- ruler
- old pair of control-top panty hose
- 2 large wiggle eyes
- pencil
- blue and green poster paint and a paintbrush
- several plastic grocery bags
- newspaper to work on
- 9-inch (23-cm) paper plate
- Styrofoam tray for drying
- masking tape
- white glue
- 12-inch (30-cm) red pipe cleaner

**1** Knot the opening of one leg of the panty hose, then cut the leg off.

**2** Knot the remaining leg off at about 12 inches (30 cms) and cut off below the knot. Stuff the partial leg with plastic grocery bags. Do not pack them too tight or you'll make the monster too heavy to stand upright on your head.

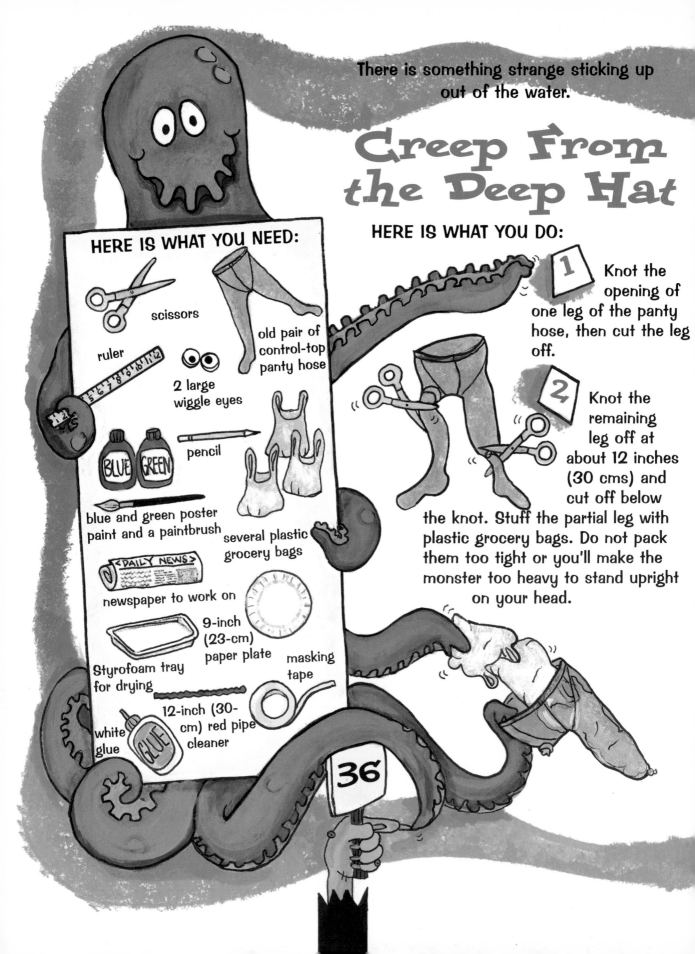

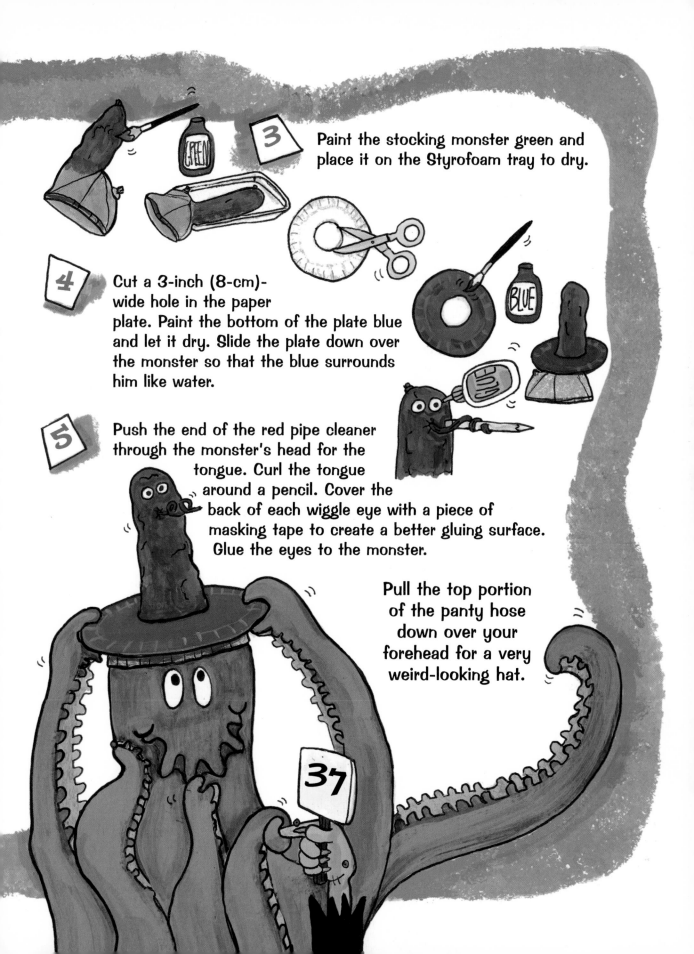

**3** Paint the stocking monster green and place it on the Styrofoam tray to dry.

**4** Cut a 3-inch (8-cm)-wide hole in the paper plate. Paint the bottom of the plate blue and let it dry. Slide the plate down over the monster so that the blue surrounds him like water.

**5** Push the end of the red pipe cleaner through the monster's head for the tongue. Curl the tongue around a pencil. Cover the back of each wiggle eye with a piece of masking tape to create a better gluing surface. Glue the eyes to the monster.

Pull the top portion of the panty hose down over your forehead for a very weird-looking hat.

37

This guy must have a very bad headache.

# Throbbing Brain Puppet

## HERE IS WHAT YOU DO:

**1** Cut the spout end off the soda bottle. Turn the bottom portion of the bottle upside down to make the head of the puppet, with the bottom of the bottle now being the top of the head.

**2** Cut the construction paper to fit around the bottom face portion of the bottle. Tape the paper around the bottle. Use the markers to draw a face and hair on the bottle.

## HERE IS WHAT YOU NEED:

scissors

2-liter plastic soda bottle

construction paper in skin color of your choice

cellophane tape

markers

colorful sock

red balloon

small detergent bottle

6-inch (15-cm) pipe cleaner

hole punch

clear plastic wrap

**3**

Cut the foot portion off the sock. Use the cuff to cover the detergent bottle.

**4**

Remove the cap from the bottle. Inflate the balloon partway and slip it over the neck of the open bottle. Let out enough air so that the balloon is inflated, but not stretched at all.

**5**

Tear off a square of plastic wrap. Arrange it around the edge of the inside top of the head of the puppet.

**6**

Slip the balloon up in the center of the head for the brain.

**7**

Punch a hole in the back bottom edge of the head of the puppet. Use the pipe cleaner to attach the head to the detergent bottle body of the puppet.

To make the brain throb, just squeeze the body of the puppet again and again.

"Oh, my aching head!"

This creature is definitely not of this world.

# Alien Necklace

**HERE IS WHAT YOU DO:**

**1** Cut a 3-inch (8-cm) piece of pipe cleaner for the arms and a 6-inch (15-cm) piece for the legs of the alien. Use the green glue to glue the arms across the center of one spoon with the bowl end at the top.

**HERE IS WHAT YOU NEED:**

scissors

ruler

12-inch (30-cm) green pipe cleaner

green craft glue

two wooden ice-cream spoons

green yarn

clamp clothespin

Styrofoam tray for drying

black construction paper scrap

**2** Fold the leg piece in half and bend each end forward to form feet for the alien. Glue the legs hanging down from the bottom of the spoon.

**3** Cut a 3-foot (1-m) length of yarn. Glue the two ends of the yarn to the top end of the spoon to make a necklace.

**4** Cover the spoon, yarn ends, and pipe cleaners (where they touch the spoon) with more glue, then place the second spoon on top of the first one. Hold the two spoons together with the clamp clothespin and let them dry on the Styrofoam tray. When dry, remove the clothespin.

**5** Color the front of the alien with green glue.

**6** Cut two eyes from the black construction paper scrap and glue them to the head of the alien.

Take me to your leader.

41

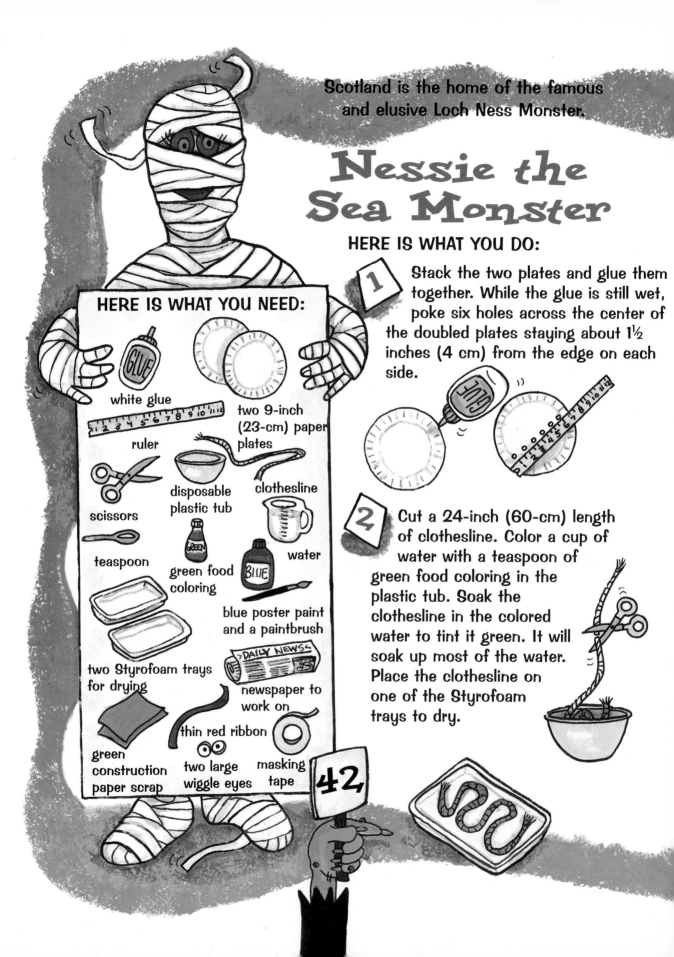

Scotland is the home of the famous and elusive Loch Ness Monster.

# Nessie the Sea Monster

## HERE IS WHAT YOU DO:

**1** Stack the two plates and glue them together. While the glue is still wet, poke six holes across the center of the doubled plates staying about 1½ inches (4 cm) from the edge on each side.

**2** Cut a 24-inch (60-cm) length of clothesline. Color a cup of water with a teaspoon of green food coloring in the plastic tub. Soak the clothesline in the colored water to tint it green. It will soak up most of the water. Place the clothesline on one of the Styrofoam trays to dry.

### HERE IS WHAT YOU NEED:

white glue

ruler

two 9-inch (23-cm) paper plates

scissors

disposable plastic tub

clothesline

teaspoon

green food coloring

water

blue poster paint and a paintbrush

two Styrofoam trays for drying

newspaper to work on

green construction paper scrap

thin red ribbon

two large wiggle eyes

masking tape

42

**3** Paint both sides of the glued plate blue to look like water. Let it dry on a Styrofoam tray.

**4** Weave the green clothesline in and out of the plate to look like a sea monster swimming through the water. Trim off any extra line.

**5** Cut two triangle-shaped pieces for the monster's tail out of the green construction paper. Glue them together over one end of the clothesline.

**6** Cut the two sides of the head for the monster from the green paper scraps. Cut a 2-inch (5-cm) length of thin red ribbon. Glue the head together with the other end of the line and the red ribbon between them. Cut a V shape out of one end of the tongue.

**7** Put a small piece of masking tape on the back of each wiggle eye to create a better gluing surface. Glue an eye on each side of the head.

Wouldn't you like to spot a sea monster?

# Monster in a Box

## HERE IS WHAT YOU DO:

**HERE IS WHAT YOU NEED:**

- small flip-top detergent box
- spray paint (BLACK)
- 2-inch (5-cm) Styrofoam ball
- scissors
- pipe cleaner pieces
- 10-inch (25-cm) stick
- adult-size green sock
- fiberfill (FIBERFILL)
- ruler
- two large wiggle eyes
- white glue (GLUE)
- two old work gloves

**1** Carefully wash any excess detergent out of the box. Do not saturate the box with water or it will fall apart. Let the box dry completely before spraying it, inside and out, with paint. (Don't use tempera paint on this type of box, as it probably will not stick well to the shiny surface.)

44

**2** Cut a hole in the bottom center of the box big enough for your hand to fit through.

**3** To make a monster, put the Styrofoam ball into the toe of the sock. Push one end of the stick up inside the sock and into the Styrofoam ball. Put fiberfill in the puppet around the stick to give the monster some shape.

**4** Cut a 4-inch (10-cm) slit on each side of the cuff of the sock. Push the sock monster up into the box from the bottom. Open the two sides of the cut cuff of the sock over the bottom of the box and glue them in place to hold the puppet in the box.

**5** Glue the two wiggle eyes on the top front of the puppet. Push the pieces of pipe cleaner into the Styrofoam ball head to add monster details to the face.

**6** Stuff the glove of the hand you will be using to work the puppet with fiberfill. Glue the stuffed hand to the bottom of the box to look like you are holding the box when your hand will actually be up in the box holding the stick to move the puppet. Put the loose glove on your other hand. Use the stick to make the monster puppet flip open the lid of the box and have a look around.

Wait a minute. If both your hands are holding the box, who is controlling the monster? Don't give away your secret!

GLUE

?

# ABOUT THE AUTHOR AND ARTIST

Twenty-five years as a teacher and director of nursery school programs in Oneida, New York, have given Kathy Ross extensive experience in guiding children through craft projects. A collector of teddy bears and paper dolls and friendly-looking monsters, her craft projects have frequently appeared in "Highlights" magazine. She is the author of three major Millbrook series: Holiday Crafts for Kids, Crafts for Kids Who Are Wild About. . ., and Crafts for All Seasons. The most recent of her more than thirty craft books for children are <u>The Best Birthday Parties Ever: A Kid's Do-It-Yourself Guide</u>, <u>Christmas Ornaments Kids Can Make</u>, and <u>Christmas Decorations Kids Can Make</u>.

Sharon Hawkins Vargo is a graduate of Pratt Institute. She lives in Carmel, Indiana, with her husband and four teenage sons. A gardener and in-line skater, she has illustrated a number of early readers. Her illustrations for <u>Carrot Stew</u> were a part of a series that won first place for art and design in its category at the New York Book Show.